THE DEATH PENALTY

POINT/COUNTERPOINT

Philosophers Debate Contemporary Issues
General Editors: James P. Sterba and Rosemarie Tong

This new series provides a philosophical angle to debates currently raging in academic and larger circles. Each book is a short volume (around 200 pages) in which two prominent philosophers debate different sides of an issue. Future topics might include the canon, the ethics of abortion rights, and pornography. For more information contact Professor Sterba, Department of Philosophy, University of Notre Dame, Notre Dame, IN 46566, or Professor Tong, Department of Philosophy, Davidson College, Davidson, NC 28036.

Political Correctness: For and Against
　　Marilyn Friedman, Washington University, St. Louis
　　Jan Narveson, University of Waterloo, Ontario, Canada
Humanitarian Intervention: Just War vs. Pacifism
　　Robert L. Phillips, University of Connecticut
　　Duane L. Cady, Hamline University
Affirmative Action: Social Justice or Unfair Preference?
　　Albert G. Mosley, Ohio University
　　Nicholas Capaldi, University of Tulsa
Religion in the Public Square: The Place of Religious Convictions in Political Debate
　　Robert Audi, University of Nebraska
　　Nicholas Wolterstorff, Yale University
Sexual Harassment: A Debate
　　Linda LeMoncheck
　　Mane Hajdin, University of Waikato
The Death Penalty: For and Against
　　Louis P. Pojman, United States Military Academy
　　Jeffrey Reiman, American University

THE DEATH PENALTY

For and Against

Louis P. Pojman
Jeffrey Reiman

ROWMAN & LITTLEFIELD PUBLISHERS, INC.
Lanham • Boulder • New York • Oxford

ROWMAN & LITTLEFIELD PUBLISHERS, INC.

Published in the United States of America
by Rowman & Littlefield Publishers, Inc.
4720 Boston Way, Lanham, Maryland 20706

12 Hid's Copse Road
Cummor Hill, Oxford OX2 9JJ, England

British Library Cataloguing in Publication Information Available

Library of Congress Cataloging-in-Publication Data

Pojman, Louis P.
　　The death penalty : for and against / Louis P. Pojman, Jeffrey
Reiman.
　　　　p.　cm.—(Point/counterpoint)
　　Includes bibliographical references and index.
　　ISBN 0-8476-8632-9 (cloth).—ISBN 0-8476-8633-7 (paper)
　　1. Capital punishment.　I. Reiman, Jeffrey H.　II. Title.
III. Series.
HV8694.P57　1998
364.66—dc21　　　　　　　　　　　　　　　　97-27795
　　　　　　　　　　　　　　　　　　　　　　　CIP

ISBN 0-8476-8632-9 (cloth : alk. paper)
ISBN 0-8476-8633-7 (pbk. : alk. paper)

Printed in the United States of America

∞ ™ The paper used in this publication meets the minimum requirements of
American National Standard for Information Sciences—Permanence of Paper for
Printed Library Materials, ANSI Z39.48–1984.

Contents

Preface and Acknowledgments   ix

1   For the Death Penalty   1
    Louis P. Pojman

2   Why the Death Penalty Should Be Abolished in America   67
    Jeffrey Reiman

3   Reply to Jeffrey Reiman   133
    Louis P. Pojman

4   Reply to Louis P. Pojman   151
    Jeffrey Reiman

Index   161

About the Authors   177

For
Hugo Adam Bedau
and
Ernest van den Haag

Preface and Acknowledgments

Today, in the United States, more than three thousand people are on death row awaiting execution. When Americans are asked in polls whether they favor the death penalty for convicted murderers, they answer overwhelmingly in the affirmative. Asked a more complicated question, such as whether they would favor life in prison without chance of parole over the death penalty, large numbers defect from the death penalty camp in favor of genuine lifetime incarceration—especially if it includes work by convicted murderers aimed at making some restitution to victims' loved ones. Likewise, since the Supreme Court gave the green light to death penalty legislation in 1976, almost every state in the union has passed laws providing capital punishment for specially grave murders. And yet, for all that, few convicted murderers get executed. Prosecutors ask for the death penalty in only a fraction of the cases in which they could, juries approve it in only a fraction of the cases in which it is asked, and a substantial number of death sentences are overturned on appeal. It seems in short that Americans are deeply ambivalent about the death penalty—they believe it's right but they're reluctant to impose it. Though such ambivalence may make life difficult for policy makers, it doesn't necessarily speak badly of Americans. They are, it seems, pulled between the noble desire to do justice and the equally worthy instinct of compassion. They are living out in the "real world" just the sort of moral conflict that philosophers try to clarify and resolve in their world of theories.

It was such a thought that led to the writing of this book. Our aim is not to replace the thinking of American citizens, but to try to identify in their full complexity the fundamental considerations that weigh for and against the death penalty, to argue forcefully on both sides of the issue so that thoughtful persons—students and citizens generally—might make use of the work that philosophers have done on this vexed topic in order to arrive at their own conclusions.

What follows is in the form of a debate: The first essay, arguing for the death penalty, was written by Louis Pojman. The second essay, arguing against the death penalty, was written by Jeffrey Reiman. These are followed by a reply to Reiman's essay by Pojman, and a reply to Pojman's essay by Reiman. Each author wrote a complete draft of his essay before seeing the other's—however, once written, each sent a copy of his essay to the other and received comments and suggestions on it. Likewise with the replies. Thus, while this was a debate, it was not a debate aimed at winning points. Each author freely offered help to the other in making the best argument for his case. And each author heartily thanks the other for that help which both authors believe improved the essays considerably. The authors also suggest that readers read this book in the same spirit in which it was written: look not to win but to figure out where the best arguments lie.

The authors are happy to thank Ernest van den Haag (who discussed this project with Louis Pojman, and who earlier debated the topic—live and in print—with Jeffrey Reiman) and Hugo Adam Bedau (who read and commented on a draft of Jeffrey Reiman's essay) for sharing with us the wisdom that each has accumulated after decades of reflection and writing on this topic. Because of their signal contributions to the philosophical discussion of the moral dimensions of capital punishment, we dedicate this book to them.

We thank as well, Jim Sterba, professor of philosophy at the University of Notre Dame and general editor (with Rosemarie Tong) of the Rowman & Littlefield series "Point/Counterpoint: Philosophers Debate Contemporary Issues," for suggesting this book and inviting the authors to write it. We hope we have lived up to the faith he showed in us. Louis Pojman also expresses his gratitude to John Kleinig, Michael Levin, and Tziporah Kasachkoff for commenting on earlier drafts of his essay. Both authors thank Cindy Nixon for her careful and intelligent editing of the manuscript.

Louis Pojman thanks his wife Trudy, and Jeffrey Reiman thanks his wife Sue Headlee, for all those things that make life and work possible and joyful and for which words are no match.

L.P. & J.R.

1

For the Death Penalty

Louis P. Pojman

Introduction

*What kind and what degree of punishment does public justice take as its
principle and norm? None other than the principle of equality in the
movement of the pointer of the scale of justice, the principle of not inclining to one side more than to the other. Thus any undeserved evil which
you do to someone else among the people is an evil done to yourself. If you
rob him, you rob yourself; if you slander him, you slander yourself; if you
strike him, you strike yourself; and if you kill him, you kill yourself.*

Immanuel Kant.[1]

On August 15, 1990, Angel Diaz, age 19, was sentenced in the Bronx for
the murder of an Israeli immigrant who had employed one of Diaz's
friends. After strangling the man with a shoelace and stabbing him, Diaz
and four friends donned Halloween masks to rob, beat, and gang-rape
the man's wife and 16-year-old daughter. The women were then sexually
tortured while the murdered man's 3-year-old daughter watched from her
crib.

Angel Diaz already had been convicted of burglary four times before he
was 16 years old. Diaz's lawyer, Paul Auerbach, said that Diaz was an

I wish to thank Ernest van den Haag for helping me get started on this project.
Robert Audi, Anthony Hartle, John Kekes, John Kleinig, Michael Levin, Stephen
Nathanson, Peter Stromberg, Jeffrey Reiman and Tziporah Kasachkoff made valu-
able suggestions and criticisms on earlier drafts of this essay.

1. Immanuel Kant, *The Metaphysics of Morals*, trans. E. Hastie (Edinburgh,
1887; originally published 1779), 155.

1

honest boy forced by poverty to do bad things. Diaz was sentenced to prison for 38 and one-third years to life on thirteen counts of murder, robbery, burglary, and conspiracy. His accomplice, Victor Sanchez, 21, who worked for the murdered man and planned the murder, had already been sentenced to 15 years to life.[2]

The National Center of Health Statistics has reported that the homicide rate for young men in the United States is four to seventy-three times the rate of other industrialized countries. In 1994, 23,330 murders were committed in the United States. Whereas killings per 100,000 by men 15 through 24 years old in 1987 was 0.3 in Austria and 0.5 in Japan, the figure was 21.9 in the United States and as high as 232 per 100,000 for blacks in some states. The nearest nation to the United States was Scotland, with a 5.0 homicide rate. In some central city areas the rate is 732 times that of men in Austria. In 1994, the rate was 37 per 100,000 men between the ages of 15 and 24.[3] The number of homicides in New York City broke the 2,000 mark in 1990. Black males in Harlem are said to have a lower life expectancy than males in Bangladesh. Escalating crime has caused an erosion in the quality of urban living. It is threatening the fabric of our social life.

Homo sapiens is the only species in which it is common for one member to kill another. In most species when there is a conflict between individuals, the weaker party submits to the stronger through some ritual gesture and is then permitted to depart in peace. Only in captivity, where the defeated animal cannot get away, will it be killed. Only human beings deliberately kill other individuals and groups of their own species. Perhaps it is not that we are more aggressive than other species but that our drives have been made more lethal by the use of weapons. A weapon, such as a gun or bomb, allows us to harm or kill without actually making physical contact with our victim. A person with a gun need not even touch his or

---

2. "Jail for Crime That Shocked Even the Jaded," *New York Times* (August 16, 1990).

3. Statistics are from the National Center of Health Statistics and are available from the Center for Disease Control. The National Center for Injury Prevention and Control reports that, in 1994, 8,116 young people aged 15 to 24 were victims of homicide. This amounts to an average of 22 youth victims per day in the United States. This homicide rate is 10 times higher than Canada's, 15 times higher than Australia's and 28 times higher than France's and Germany's. In 1994 in the United States 102,220 rapes and 618,950 robberies were reported.

her victim. Someone who sends a letter bomb through the mail may never have even laid eyes on the victim. The inhibition against killing is undermined by the trigger's power, a point to be kept in mind when discussing gun-control legislation. Airplane bomber pilots need not even see their victims as they press the button unleashing destruction. We are a violent race whose power of destruction has increased in proportion to our technology.

Naturally, the subject of punishment should receive increased attention, as should the social causes of crime. As a radical student activist in the 1960s, I once opposed increased police protection for my neighborhood in Morningside Heights, New York City, arguing that we must get to the causes of crime rather than deal only with the symptoms. I later realized that this was like refusing fire fighters the use of water hoses to put out fires because they only dealt with the symptoms rather than the causes of the fire.

The truth is that we do not know the exact nature of what causes crimes of violence. Males commit a disproportionate number of violent crimes in our country, over 90 percent. Why is this? In fact young black males (between the ages of 15 and 24) constitute the group with the greatest tendency towards violent crimes.[4] Many people in the United States believe that *poverty causes crime*, but this is false. Poverty is a terrible condition, and surely contributes to crime, but it is not a necessary or sufficient condition for violent crime. The majority of people in India are far poorer than most of the American poor, yet a person, male or female, can walk through the worst slum of Calcutta or New Delhi at any time of the day or night without fearing molestation. As a student I lived in a very poor neighborhood in a city in England which was safer than the Midwestern middle-class neighborhood in which I grew up. The use and trafficking of illegal drugs contributes to a great deal of crime, and the turn from heroin to crack as the "drug of choice" has exacerbated the matter, but plenty of crime occurred in our society before drugs became the problem they now are. Thus we leave the subject of the causes of crime for psychologists and sociologists to solve and turn to the nature of punishment.

---

4. The United States 1994 *Uniform Crime Report* states that 1,864,168 violent crimes occurred in 1994; 25,052 offenders were listed. "Of those whom sex and age were reported 91% of the offenders were males, and 84% were persons 18 years of age or older. . . . Of offenders for whom race was known, 56% were black, 42% white, and the remainder were persons of other races" (p. 14).

My discussion will be divided into two parts. In Part I, I discuss the major theories of punishment, preparing the way for a discussion of capital punishment. In Part II, I argue that a proper understanding of the nature of punishment justifies capital punishment for some crimes.

Part I: Punishment

To be responsible for a past act is to be liable to praise or blame. If the act was especially good, we go further than praise. We reward it. If it was especially evil, we go further than blame. We punish it. In order to examine the notion of punishment and then that of capital punishment, we first need to inquire under what conditions, if any, criminal punishment is justified. We will look at three approaches to this problem: the retributivist, the utilitarian, and the rehabilitationist.

Even though few of us will ever become criminals or be indicted on criminal charges, most of us feel very strongly about the matter of criminal punishment. Something about crime touches the deepest nerves of our imagination. Take the following situations, which are based on newspaper reports from the mid-1990s:

(1) A drug addict in New York City stabs to death a vibrant, gifted, 22-year-old graduate student who has dedicated her life to helping others.

(2) A sex-pervert lures little children into his home, sexually abuses them, and then kills them. Over twenty bodies are discovered on his property.

(3) A man sends his wife and daughter on an airplane trip, puts a time bomb into their luggage, and takes out a million dollar insurance policy on them. The money will be used to pay off his gambling debts and for prostitutes.

(4) A bomb explodes outside the Alfred P. Murrah Federal Building in Oklahoma City, killing more than 160 people and injuring many others.

What is it within us that rises up in indignation at the thought of these atrocities? What should happen to the criminals in these cases? How can the victims (or their loved ones) ever be compensated for these crimes? We feel conflicting emotional judgments of harsh vengeance toward the criminal and, at the same time, concern that we don't ourselves become violent and irrational in our quest for revenge.

The Definition of Punishment

We may define "punishment," or, more precisely, "institutional or legal punishment," as *an evil inflicted by a person in a position of authority upon another person who is judged to have violated a rule.*[5] It can be analyzed into five concepts:

1. *An evil:* To punish is to inflict harm, unpleasantness, or suffering (not necessarily pain). Regarding this concept, the question is: Under what conditions is it right to cause harm or inflict suffering?
2. *For a violation:* The violation is either a moral or a legal offense. The pertinent questions are: Should we punish everyone who commits a moral offense? Need the offense already have been committed or may we engage in preemptive punishment where we have good evidence that the agent will commit a crime?
3. *Done to the offender:* The offender must be judged or believed to be guilty of a crime. Does this rule out the possibility of punishing innocent people? What should we call the process of "framing" the innocent and "punishing" them?
4. *Carried out by a personal agency.*
5. *Imposed by an authority.*

Let us spend a moment examining each of these points and the questions they raise.

1. Punishment is an evil. It may involve corporal punishment, loss of rights or freedom, or even loss of life. These are things we normally condemn as immoral. How does what is normally considered morally wrong suddenly become morally right? To quote H. L. A. Hart, former Oxford University professor of jurisprudence, What is this "mysterious piece of moral alchemy in which the combination of two evils of moral wickedness and suffering are transmuted into good"?[6] Theories of punishment bear

---

5. In the following analysis I am indebted to Anthony Flew, "Justification of Punishment," *Philosophy* (1954); Joel Feinberg, "Punishment," *Philosophy of Law*, 2nd ed., eds. Joel Feinberg and Hyman Gross (Wadsworth, 1980); and Herbert Morris, "Persons and Punishment," *The Monist* 52 (October 1968). See also Tziporah Kasachkoff, "The Criteria of Punishment: Some Neglected Considerations," *Canadian Journal of Philosophy* 2, no. 3 (March 1973).

6. H. L. A. Hart, *Punishment and Responsibility* (Oxford University Press, 1968), 234.

the burden of proof to justify why punishment is required. The three classical theories have been retribution, deterrence, and rehabilitation (or reform of the criminal). We shall examine each of these below. These theories attempt not only to justify types of punishment, but also to provide guidance on the degrees of punishment to be given for various crimes and persons.

2. Punishment is given for an offense, but must it be for a violation of a legal statute or may it also be for any moral failure? While most legal scholars agree that the law should have a moral basis, it is impractical to make laws against every moral wrong. If we had a law against lying, for example, our courts would be cluttered beyond our ability. Also some laws may be immoral (e.g., anti-abortionists believe that the laws permitting abortion are immoral), but they still are laws, carrying with them coercive measures.

Whether we should punish only offenses already committed or also crimes that are intended is a difficult question. If I know or have good evidence that Smith is about to kill some innocent child (but not which one), and the only way to prevent this is by incarcerating Smith (or killing him), why isn't this morally acceptable? Normally, we don't have certainty about people's intentions, so we can't be certain that Smith really means to kill the child. But what if we do have strong evidence in this case? Nations sometimes launch preemptive strikes when they have strong evidence of an impending attack (e.g., Israel in the Six-Day War in 1967 acted on reliable information that Arab nations were going to attack it. It launched a preemptive strike that probably saved many Israeli lives). Although preemptive strikes are about defense, not punishment per se, could the analogy carry over? After all, part of the role of punishment is defense against future crimes.

This is a difficult subject, and I can conceive of conditions under which we would incapacitate would-be criminals before they commit their crimes, but the opportunity for abuse is so enormous here that one needs to tread carefully. In general our laws permit punishing only the guilty, relying on the principle that every dog may have its first bite—or, at least, an attempt at a first bite.

3. Punishment is done to the offender. No criminologist justifies punishing the innocent, but classic cases of framing the innocent in order to maximize utility exist. Sometimes Caiaphus's decision to frame and execute Jesus of Nazareth (John 10:50) is cited. "It were better that one man

should die for a nation than that the whole nation perish." Utilitarians seem to be vulnerable to such practices, but every utilitarian philosopher of law eschews such egregious miscarriages of justice. Why this is so is a point I will discuss below.

This stipulation, "done to an offender," also rules out other uses of the word "punish," as when, for instance, we say that boxer Mike Tyson "punished" his opponent with a devastating left to the jaw. Such metaphorical or non-legal uses of the term are excluded from our analysis. Similarly, we quarantine confirmed or potential disease carriers, but we would not call this imposed suffering "punishment," for our intention is not to cause suffering (but to prevent it) and the carrier is innocent of any wrongdoing.

4. Punishment is carried out by a Personal agency. Punishment is not the work of natural forces but of people. Lightning may strike and kill a criminal, but only people (or conscious beings) can punish other people.

5. Punishment is imposed by an Authority. Punishment is conferred through institutions which have to do with maintaining laws or social codes. This rules out vigilante executions as punishments. Only a recognized authority, such as the state, can carry out legal punishment for criminal behavior.

We turn now to the leading theories on punishment.

Theories of Punishment

Retributivist Theories

Retributivist theories make infliction of punishment dependent upon what the agent, as a wrong-doer, deserves, rather than on any future social utility which might result from the infliction of suffering on the criminal. That is, rather than focusing on any *future* good that might result from punishment, retributivist theories are *backward* looking, assessing the nature of the misdeed. The most forceful proponents of this view are Immanuel Kant (1724–1804), C. S. Lewis (1898–1963), and Herbert Morris. Here is a classic quotation from Kant, which deserves to be quoted at length:

> Juridical punishment can never be administered merely as a means for promoting another good either with regard to the criminal himself or to civil

society, but must in all cases be imposed only because the individual on whom it is inflicted *has committed a crime*. For one man ought never to be dealt with merely as a means subservient to the purpose of another, nor be mixed up with the subjects of real right. Against such treatment his inborn personality has a right to protect him, even though he may be condemned to lose his civil personality. He must first be found guilty and *punishable* before there can be any thought of drawing from his punishment any benefit for himself or his fellow-citizens.

The principle of punishment is a categorical imperative, and woe to him who creeps through the serpent-windings of utilitarianism to discover some advantage that may discharge him from the justice of punishment, or even reduces its amount by the advantage it promises, in accordance with the Pharisaical maxim, "It is better for *one* man to die than for an entire people to perish" [John 10:51]. For if justice and righteousness perish, there is no longer any value in men's living on the earth.

But what kind and what amount of punishment is it that public justice makes its principle and standard? It is the principle of equality, by which the pointer of the scale of justice is made to incline no more to the one side than the other. It may be rendered by saying that the undeserved evil which any one commits on another, is to be regarded as perpetrated on himself. Hence it may be said, "If you slander another, you slander yourself; if you steal from another you steal from yourself; if you strike another, you strike yourself; if you kill another, you kill yourself." This is the *law of retribution (jus talionis)*—it being understood, of course, that this is applied by a court as distinguished from private judgment. It is the only principle that can definitely assign both the quality and the quantity of a just penalty. All other standards are wavering and uncertain; and on account of other considerations involved in them, they contain no principle conformable to the sentence of pure and strict justice.

But what does it mean to say, If you steal from someone, you steal from yourself? Whoever steals makes the property of everyone else insecure and therefore deprives himself (by the principle of retribution) of security in any possible property. He has nothing and can also acquire nothing; but he still wants to live, and this is now possible if others provide for him. But since the state will not provide for him free of charge, he must let it have his powers for any kind of work it pleases (in convict or prison labor) and is reduced to the status of a slave for a certain time, or permanently if the state sees fit. If, however, he has committed murder he must *die*. Here there is no substitute that will satisfy justice. There is no similarity between life, however wretched it may be, and death, hence no likeness between the crime and the retribution unless death is judicially carried out upon the wrongdoer, although it must still be freed from any mistreatment that could make the humanity in the person suffering it into something abominable. Even if a civil society resolved to dissolve itself with the consent of all its members—as might be supposed in the case of a people inhabiting an island resolving to separate and scatter themselves throughout the whole world—the last murderer lying in prison ought to be executed before the resolution was carried out. This ought to be done in order that every one may realize the desert of his deeds, and that bloodguiltiness may not remain upon the people; for otherwise they will all be regarded as participators in the murder as a public violation of justice.[7]

This is a classic expression of the retributivist position, for it bases punishment solely on the issue of whether or not the subject in question has committed a crime and punishes him accordingly. All other considerations—eudaimonistic or utilitarian—are to be rejected as irrelevant to punishment. For example, Kant considers the possibility of a capital criminal allowing himself to be a subject in a medical experiment as a substitute for capital punishment in order to benefit the society. He rejects the suggestion. "A court would reject with contempt such a proposal from a medical college, for justice ceases to be justice if it can be bought for any price whatsoever." I have heard the phrase "that bloodguiltiness may not remain upon the people" interpreted as implying utilitarian consideration, signifying that the people will be cursed in the future. Perhaps a more charitable interpretation is that failure to punish constitutes an endorsement of the criminal act and thus a kind of criminal complicity after the act.[8]

Kant and the classic retributivist position in general have three theses about the justification of punishment:

1. Guilt is a necessary condition for judicial punishment; that is, *only* the guilty may be punished.
2. Guilt is a sufficient condition for judicial punishment; that is, *all* the guilty must be punished. If you have committed a crime, morality demands that you suffer an evil for it.
3. The correct amount of punishment imposed upon the morally (or legally) guilty offender is that amount which is *equal* to the moral seriousness of the offense.

There are various ways of arguing for these theses. One is to argue, as Kant does, that in lying, stealing, unjustly striking, or killing another, the

---

7. Immanuel Kant, *The Metaphysics of Morals* (1779), trans. E. Hastie (Edinburgh, 1887), 155–56.

8. I am grateful to Jeffrey Reiman for pointing this out to me.

offender lies, steals, unjustly strikes or kills himself. That is, by universaliz-
ing the maxim of such acts, the offender wills a like action on himself. This
is the law of retaliation (*jus talionis*). "The undeserved evil which anyone
commits on another is to be regarded as perpetuated on himself." The
criminal need not consciously desire the same punishment, but by acting
on such a principle, for example, "murder your enemies," the offender
implicitly draws the same treatment on himself. He deserves to suffer in
the same way he has harmed another. Or, at least, the suffering should be
equal and similar to the suffering he has caused. This is the *strict equality*
(sometimes called the "*lex talionis*") interpretation of retributivism.

The weakness of the equality interpretation is that it is both impractical
and impossible to inflict the very same kind of suffering on the offender as
he has imposed on others. Our social institutions are not equipped to
measure the exact amount of harm done by offenders or repay them in
kind. We rightly shrink from torturing the torturer or resuscitating the
serial murderer so that we can "kill" him a second, a third, a fourth time,
and so forth. How do you give a trusted member of the FBI or CIA who
betrays his country by spying for the enemy an equivalent harm? Our legal
systems are not equipped to punish according to the harm inflicted but,
rather, according to the wrong done, measured against specified statutes
with prescribed penalties.

A second way, following Herbert Morris and Michael Davis, is to inter-
pret these theses in terms of social equilibrium.[9] The criminal has violated
a mutually beneficial scheme of social cooperation, thereby treating law-
abiding members of the community unfairly. Punishment restores the
scales of justice, the social equilibrium of benefits and burdens. We might
put the argument this way.

1. In breaking a primary rule of society, a person obtains an unfair advantage over others.
2. Unfair advantages ought to be redressed by society if possible.
3. Punishment is a form of redressing the unfair advantage.
4. Therefore, we ought to punish the offender for breaking the primary
   rule.

---

9. Herbert Morris, "Persons and Punishment." See also Michael Davis,
"Harm and Retribution," *Philosophy & Public Affairs* 15, no. 3 (Summer 1986).

Punishment restores the social equilibrium of burdens and benefits by taking from the agent what he or she unfairly got and now owes, that is, exacting his or her debt. This argument, like the Kantian one above, holds that society has a duty to punish the offender, since society has a general duty to redress "unfair advantages if possible." That is, we have a prima facie duty to eliminate unfair advantages in society, even though that duty may be overridden by other considerations such as the high cost (financially or socially) of doing so or the criminal's repentance.

While the Kantian interpretation focuses on the nature and gravity of the harm done by the offender, Morris's *Unfair Advantage* or *Fair Play Argument* focuses on the unfairness of the offense—the idea of unfair advantage which ought to be repaid to society. Although it is not always the case that the criminal gains an advantage or profit in crime, he or she does abandon the common burden of self-restraint in order to obtain criminal ends. While the rest of us are forgoing the use of unlawful and immoral means to obtain our goals, while we are restraining ourselves from taking these shortcuts, the criminal makes use of these means to his or her ends. As such we have been unfairly taken advantage of, and justice requires the annulment of the unfair advantage. The criminal must repay his or her debt to society. He or she need not be punished in the same way as his or her offense, but the punishment must "fit the crime," be a proportionate response.

It is not clear, however, that Morris's and Davis's interpretation can do all the work. For one thing it is modeled on the act of stealing (or cheating), getting an unfair advantage over others. The criminal may obtain an unfair advantage over others by cheating on exams or taxes, by killing a rival for a job, or by stealing another's purse, but this model of unfair advantage doesn't work as well with sadistic crimes which may leave the criminal psychologically worse off than the victim. The successful rapist may be worse off, not better off, than before his crime. The terrorist who detonates a bomb on the crowded bus he is riding doesn't gain any advantage over others, for he no longer exists. Furthermore, we do not punish all instances of unfair advantage, as when someone lies. Daniel Farrell has objected to the Fair Play Argument, pointing out that even before we enter into a social contract, even in a Lockean state of nature, the concept of just desert holds, and we should intervene on behalf of an innocent victim who is being attacked by an aggressor, a malicious rapist or a killer.[10] Moreover, we think someone is deserving of punishment even when he only *attempts*—with malice aforethought—to harm others, when his intention to do evil is unsuccessful. This is sometimes referred to as *mens rea:* having a guilty mind.

Desert

Both the *Strict Equality* (*lex talionis*) and the *Fair Play* interpretations of retributivism have some validity, but both partially misfire. Strict Equality of punishment is not practical or necessary for retributive justice. On the other hand, the Fair Play argument overemphasizes the advantage gained by the criminal and fails to account for evil intentions, *mens rea*. But both theories correctly point to the broader, underlying ground for punishment: that the criminal deserves suffering in a way fitting his or her crime. Farrell correctly points to this salient feature—*desert*, which exists even in a Lockean state of nature (a precontractual state). While it is not practical, let alone necessary, to punish the criminal in a manner equal to the gravity of the crime, we can punish him or her in a manner proportionate to the seriousness of the offense. So we should modify the third premise of the Strict Equality interpretation to read:

3. The correct amount of punishment imposed upon the morally (or legally) guilty offender is that amount which is proportionate to the moral seriousness of the offense.

The concept of desert has been attacked or, more accurately, downplayed and ignored. John Rawls has asserted that there is no natural desert (for our relative superiority in talents—even the ability to make an effort is a product of heredity and family background). Since we do not deserve our natural endowments and families, we do not deserve what these things produce, our good or bad deeds.[11] Stanley Benn and R. S. Peters have denied any legitimacy to the claims that the virtuous deserve to prosper and the guilty deserve to suffer (let alone that they deserve to suffer in proportion to the gravity of their offenses). They write, "The utilitarian

---

10. Daniel Farrell, "Justification of General Deterrence," *Philosophical Review* XCIV, no. 3 (July 1985).

11. John Rawls, *A Theory of Justice* (Cambridge: Harvard University Press, 1971), 74, 100–105.

can only point out . . . that a great many people think that punishment requires some justification . . . and that though it is intolerable that there should be murder, rape, and dope-peddling, punishment is just one way of reducing the incidence of such admitted evils. He sees nothing intrinsically fitting about this particular way, which itself involves increasing the misery in the world."[12] Robert Goodin holds that *need* overrides desert in a theory of justice. He asks us to suppose that two men have been in an automobile accident and have the same serious injury, but one is guilty of the gross recklessness that caused the accident, while the other is an innocent victim. Who should get priority treatment in the emergency room? Goodin asserts that even if everyone has clear knowledge of the facts, it would be outrageous to give preferential treatment to the innocent victim.[13]

I think that desert deserves a better defense.

The concept of desert is connected with our notion of responsibility. As free agents who can choose, a moral universe would be so arranged that we would be rewarded or punished in a manner equal to our virtue or vice. As the ancient adage puts it, "Whatsoever a man sows that shall he also reap." Those who sow good deeds would reap good results, and those who choose to sow their wild oats would reap accordingly. Given a notion of objective morality, the good should prosper and the evil should suffer— both in equal measure to their virtue or vice. This idea is reflected in the Eastern idea of karma: You will be repaid in the next life for what you did in this one. The ancient Greek philosophers and the Roman jurists, beginning with Cicero, define justice as giving to each his due, *suum cuique tribuens.* Jesus may be seen as adumbrating the same principle in his statement, "Render unto Caesar that which is Caesar's and unto God that which is God's" (Luke 20:25). In the Christian tradition it is reflected in the doctrine of heaven and hell (and purgatory). The good will be rewarded according to their good works and the evil will be punished in hell—which they have chosen by their actions. Leibniz put the matter thusly:

> Thus it is that the pains of the damned continue, even when they no longer serve to turn them away from evil, and that likewise the rewards of the blessed

---

12. Stanley Benn and R. S. Peters, "The Utilitarian Case for Deterrence," in *Contemporary Punishment*, eds. Rudolph Gerber and Patrick McAnany (University of Notre Dame Press, 1972), 97–98.

13. Robert Goodin, "Negating Positive Desert Claims," *Political Theory* 13, no. 4 (November 1985): 574–98.

continue, even when they no longer serve for strengthening them in good. One may say nevertheless that the damned ever bring upon themselves new pains through new sins, and that the blessed ever bring upon themselves new joys by new progress in goodness: for both are founded on the *principle of the fitness of things*, which has seen to it that affairs were so ordered that the evil action must bring upon itself chastisement.[14]

It would seem that eternal hell is excessive punishment for human evil and eternal bliss excessive reward, but the basic idea of *moral fittingness* seems to make sense. Leibniz is referring to the same principle which Kant, as noted above, calls the principle of *equality*, a sort of symmetry between input and output in any endeavor. We get a hint of this symmetry in the practice of gratitude. We normally and spontaneously feel grateful for services rendered. Someone treats us to dinner, gives us a present, teaches us a skill, rescues us from a potential disaster or simply gives us directions. A sense of gratitude wells up inside of us toward our benefactor. We feel indebted, a sense of obligation toward him or her. We sense we have a duty to reciprocate in kind. On the other hand, if someone intentionally and cruelly hurts us, deceives us, betrays our trust, we feel involuntary resentment. We want to reciprocate and harm that person. The offender deserves to be harmed, and we have a right to harm him. If he has harmed someone else, we have an instinctual duty to harm him. Henry Sidgwick argued that these basic emotions are in fact the grounds for our notion of desert: Punishment is resentment universalized and rewards—a sort of positive retribution—gratitude universalized.[15] Whether such a reduction of desert to resentment and gratitude completely explains our notion of desert may be questioned, but it lends support to two theses: first, that there is natural, pre-institutional desert and, second, that desert creates obligations.

John Rawls has influenced a number of social and political thinkers with his suggestion that natural desert does not exist; rather, desert originates a contractual situation (for Rawls, behind the veil of ignorance), where parties to the contract consider fair practices. Desert must be tied to institutions, which may decide to reward and punish in ways that are based on basic principles. But this idea seems to put the cart before the horse.

---

14. G. W. Leibniz, *Theodicy* (trans. E. M. Huggard), 1698.
15. Henry Sidgwick, *Methods of Ethics* (Hackett Publishing Company), bk. III, chap. 5.

Rather than society inventing desert, desert grounds a just society. It is the measure of whether a society is just or unjust. Desert is not invented by society but discovered as a moral requirement, without which the society itself lacks justification.

These reactions of gratitude and resentment are primitive and natural. They are seen in animal behavior as well as in the most primitive human societies. The chimpanzee who is groomed by another chimpanzee will come to the aid of his benefactor. Wolves will kill unreliable members of their pack, who threaten their well-being. Rather than detractors from justice, these primordial reactions may be the grounds of justice, an Ur-justice.

This primordial desert-based idea of justice has two parts: Every action in the universe has a fitting response in terms of creating a duty to punish or reward, and that response must be *appropriate* in measure to the original action. It follows that evil deeds must be followed by evil outcomes and good deeds by good outcomes, exactly equal or in proportion to the vice or virtue in question. That is the basis of a primordial meritocracy, recognized in all cultures and religions but denied or undermined by much of contemporary political philosophy.

I cannot prove this principle to you. It is a basic principle, more certain to me than any of the proofs that would support it. I can only ask you to reflect on the nature of desert and determine whether you see it the same way. If you agree that people deserve the results of their voluntary deeds, then do we not have an obligation to enable them to receive their deserts? Consider this situation: Jane is a devoted wife who puts her husband Jack through medical school, working long hours and sacrificing her education for him. Jack is so fully caught up in his medical studies that he fails to be grateful to Jane for all she is doing. Upon graduating with his M.D., with a lucrative practice in hand, Jack announces to Jane that he has found a younger woman and will be divorcing her. Doesn't Jane deserve an ample alimony, and doesn't Jack deserve not only our censure, but also to have some of his earnings transferred to Jane? Doesn't Jane have a moral claim on Jack which society in general should help enforce?

Or consider two equally talented young adults, Bob and Bill. Bob is a lazy scoundrel. He cheated his way through school, sponges off his friends without feeling the least gratitude, spends his time surfing off the Santa Monica coast, and makes no positive contribution to his community. Bill, on the other hand, not only studied hard for his college degree, but spent his weekends helping to educate poor children. He has lived an exemplary moral life, striving to contribute to the welfare of his community. Through no fault of his own, he has been laid off by a large company that is downsizing. Both Bob and Bill are now in need of your financial help, but you have the means to help only one of them. Who should you help? Doesn't Bill have a general claim to society's help? Doesn't his deserving good create an obligation on us to help him? The obligation is overridden if we lack the resources to help Bill or if we have other duties that take precedence over this one. Bob doesn't deserve our help, but if we have additional resources, we might, nevertheless, choose to help him—hoping to reform him. Our duty to give Bob what he deserves may be overridden by mercy or utility (e.g., we think Bob could make a great surfing instructor for children). But if our best judgment convinces us that Bob will not reform, we may choose to give him what he deserves, which is no help at all.

The same notion of desert-as-creating-obligations underlies our revulsion against prejudicial discrimination. We object to racist and sexist practices because they treat people unfairly: they make irrelevant features, such as race and gender, rather than desert or merit, the criteria for social goods. We have a duty not to harm people unjustly (i.e., not to inflict undeserved harm on them), but we treat them positively according to their moral dignity. Similarly, children who have been afflicted with life-threatening diseases deserve to be compensated by society so that their undeserved suffering is mitigated. Such desert claims create prima facie obligations on all of us who have the means to aid them. This principle seems to be one that is intuitively recognized by people everywhere in their everyday practices. The sociologist George Caspar Homans has noted that in economic relations people in every culture "are alike in holding the notion of proportionality between investment and profit that lies at the heart of distributive justice" and have a notion that "fair exchange . . . is realized when the profit, or reward less cost, of each man is directly proportional to his investment."[16]

Desert and Utilitarianism

One can partially explain our belief in the propriety of rewarding and punishing people according to the nature of their acts by utilitarian consid-

---

16. George Caspar Homans, *Social Behavior: Its Elementary Forms* (Routledge & Kegan Paul, 1961), 246, 264.

erations. Rewarding good works encourages further good works, while punishment has a deterrent effect. By recognizing and rewarding merit, we promote efficiency and welfare. We want the very best generals to lead our sons and daughters to battle, the most outstanding basketball and football players to play on our team, and excellent surgeons, airline pilots, and judges to serve our needs. A superior teacher can teach twice or thrice as effectively as a minimally competent one. We want the best car for our money, not just an average car. While some tasks have thresholds beyond which it is not necessary to improve on (e.g., I'm satisfied with our slow mail delivery, though getting the mail a few hours earlier would be better), some tasks—those mentioned above—crucially depend upon high efficiency. So a utilitarian defense of general meritocracy is possible. In general we can say that a society that has a fitting notion of rewarding those who contribute to its well-being and punishing those who work against its well-being will survive and prosper better than a society lacking these practices. But, of course, utilitarian considerations can be used to override considerations of merit.

Utilitarian considerations are important, but I doubt that they are the whole story behind the long-standing, universal history of our faith in meritocracy. One would like to have a non-utilitarian, *deontological* argument to ground our intuitions that regarding any good and useful function X, the good (at X) should prosper and the bad (at X) should suffer. W. D. Ross argues that meritocracy is a fundamental intuition, offering, as evidence for this thesis, the following thought experiment. After identifying two intrinsically good things (1) pleasure and (2) virtue, Ross asks us to consider a third:

> If we compare two imaginary states of the universe, alike in the total amounts of virtue and vice and of pleasure and pain present in the two, but in one of which the virtuous were all happy and the vicious miserable, while in the other the virtuous were miserable and the vicious happy, very few people would hesitate to say that the first was a much better state of the universe than the second. It would seem then that, besides virtue and pleasure, we must recognize (3), as a third independent good, the apportionment of pleasure and pain to the virtuous and the vicious respectively. And it is on the recognition of this as a separate good that the recognition of the duty of justice, in distinction from fidelity to promise on the one hand and from beneficence on the other, rests.[17]

---

17. W. D. Ross, *The Right and the Good* (Oxford University Press, 1930), 138.

I think that most people would agree with Ross that it is intuitively obvious that the appropriate distribution of happiness and unhappiness should be according to virtue and vice. Even if we could produce more aggregate happiness or welfare by making the vicious better off, would we not prefer a world where people get what they deserve to one of utility? Part of what makes the world good consists in giving people what they deserve. It seems to be exactly the intuition that motivated Kant's dictum that conscientiousness or the good will, being the single desert base, is the only moral basis for happiness: "An impartial spectator can never feel approval in contemplating the uninterrupted prosperity of a being graced by no touch of a pure and good will, and that consequently a good will seems to constitute the indispensable condition of our very worthiness to be happy."[18]

Consider again Farrell's example concerning an aggressor who is attacking an innocent victim in the state of nature. Would we not intervene on behalf of the victim if we thought we could safely make a difference in the outcome? Would we not think it better that the aggressor die than that the victim die? And if two aggressors attacked one victim, so that twice as many *dolors* (units of suffering) were incurred by killing both aggressors in saving the life of the innocent party, would we not prefer this than that the victim die (with the result that half as many dolors resulted)? If the correct answer to these questions is "yes," then not only is desert preinstitutional (contra Rawls and company), but it is a valid concept apart from utilitarian outcomes. If this is so, desert trumps utility.

It also trumps equality. What we object to in inequalities, I think, is that they so often are undeserved. We don't morally object when the better quarterback is chosen as a starter over ourselves, or when a superior student, who works equally hard, gets a higher grade than ourselves, or when an enterprising entrepreneur succeeds in establishing a socially useful business and thereby makes more money than his lazy brother who spends his days surfing off the California coast. What we may object to is the lazy brother inheriting vast sums of money from his enterprising brother, and what we certainly do object to is the lazy brother stealing the money from his brother, for the lazy surfer doesn't deserve his gains.

---

18. Immanuel Kant, *Groundwork of the Metaphysic of Morals*, trans. H. J. Paton (Hutchinson University Library, 1948), 59. For a fuller defense of the thesis that desert creates obligations see my "Merit: Why Do We Value It?" (forthcoming in *Journal of Social Philosophy*).

In sum, our concept of justice includes notions of responsibility, reciprocity, and desert that are preinstitutional and deontological, so that perpetrators of evil deserve to suffer and virtuous people deserve a level of well-being corresponding to their virtue. Since we have a general duty to strive to bring about justice in the world, it follows that we have a duty to try to bring it about directly or indirectly, through just institutions, by which, wherever possible, the virtuous are rewarded with well-being and the vicious with suffering, inclining them to repentance.

This is not to argue that we must always give people what they deserve. There may be grounds for mercy, forgiveness, and rehabilitation: mitigating circumstances may be taken into consideration to lessen the severity of the punishment. But the aim is to bring about moral homeostasis, a social order where the good are rewarded and the bad are punished in proportion to their deeds.

Although we have indirectly addressed it, let us say a word about the third thesis of retribution, stated earlier:

3. The correct amount of punishment imposed upon the morally (or legally) guilty offender is that amount which is proportionate to the moral seriousness of the offense.

The *lex talionis*—"an eye for an eye, a tooth for a tooth, a life for a life" (Exod. 21) set forth by Moses in the Old Testament—was actually a gesture of restraint on the passion for vengeance: A life for an eye or a tooth, two lives for the life of one member of my family. Thomas Jefferson was one of the earliest Americans to set forth a system of proportionality of punishment to crime:

> Whosoever shall be guilty of rape, polygamy, sodomy with man or woman, shall be punished, if a man, by castration, if a woman by cutting through the cartilage of her nose a hole of one half inch in diameter at the least. [And] whosoever shall maim another, or shall disfigure him . . . shall be maimed, or disfigured in the like sort: or if that cannot be, for want of some part, then as nearly as may be, in some other part of at least equal value.[19]

19. Thomas Jefferson, *Bill for Proportioning Crime and Punishments* (1779) quoted in Ernest van den Haag, *Punishing Criminals: Concerning a Very Old and Painful Question* (Basic Books, 1975), 193.

This attempt at proportionality seems to be universal. As Émile Durkheim noted, "There is no society where the rule does not exist that the punishment must be proportioned to the offense."[20] We have a general idea of *ordinal* orderings of general crimes according to their gravity, for example (1) murder; (2) rape; (3) theft; (4) perjury—but it is difficult, if not impossible, to give them absolute rankings: for example, "Theft must always be visited with 1 year in prison; burglary, with breaking and entering, with 5 years; perjury with six months," and so on, for it is hard to compare crimes. How much worse is rape than assault? Well, different rapes are of different magnitudes of severity, and likewise with assaults and murders and perjuries and so forth. Some relativity applies to our perceptions of the seriousness of crimes, so that if legal punishment is perceived as excessive, juries will fail to convict; and if legal punishment is perceived as being too lenient, private vengeance will emerge. In either case, the law is subverted. So even if it were the case that rapists deserved castration (as Jefferson advocated) or being raped themselves, if the public perception is that these punishments are too brutal, then the penal system is forced to impose lesser or, at least, different punishments. Complete punitive justice, even if we knew what it was, may not be possible in an imperfect world.

None of this is meant to deny in the least the general thesis that the punishment should fit the crime, that the criminal deserves punishment commensurate to the gravity of the crime. The discussion is meant to urge caution, restraint, a sense of our fallibility, and a realization that an insistence on perfect justice is counterproductive (*summum justicia, summa injuria*—the demand for nothing less than *perfect* justice results in perfect injury). On the other hand, we must seek to respect the demands of impartial justice, inflicting punishments that correspond to the gravity of the crime. Someone who takes another's life in cold blood (*mens rea*), deserves to die, someone who maliciously blinds another deserves blindness or something equivalent, someone who steals from another deserves to lose his possessions or—if he has gambled or spent them—to be punished in a manner deemed suitable by the judicial system (say, a certain length in prison). Roughly equivalent punishments satisfy the notion of symmetry or fittingness inherent in our notion of desert. But not all crimes (e.g., embezzlement and perjury) lend themselves to this symmetry model.

---

20. Émile Durkheim, *The Rules of Sociological Method*, (Oxford University Press, 1952) quoted in van den Haag, *Punishing Criminals*, 194.

out solving it. Suppose we call "punishment" punishing the guilty and give another name, such as "telishment" (Rawls's suggestion), to judicially harming the innocent for deterrent purposes. Now the question becomes "Should we ever telish people?" The utilitarian is committed to telishment—whenever the aggregate utility warrants it.

While these criticisms are severe, they do not overthrow utilitarianism altogether. One surely admits that penal law should have a deterrent effect. The point seems to be that utilitarian theories need a retributive base on which to build. I will comment on this point later.

Rehabilitative Theories

According to rehabilitative theories, crime is a disease, and the criminal is a sick person who needs to be cured, not punished. Such rehabilitationists as B. F. Skinner, Karl Menninger, and Benjamin Karpman point to the failure and cruelties of our penal system and advocate an alternative of therapy and reconditioning. "Therapy not torture" might be said to be their motto for criminals are not really in control of their behavior but are suffering personality disorders. Crime is, by and large, a result of an adverse early environment, so that what must be done is to recondition the criminal through positive reinforcement. Punishment is a prescientific response to antisocial behavior. At best punishment temporarily suppresses adverse behavior, but, if untreated, Skinner argues, it will resurface again as though the punishment never occurred. It is useless as a deterrent. Rehabilitationists charge that retributivists are guilty of holding an antiquated notion of human beings as possessing free wills and being responsible for their behavior. We, including all of our behavior, are all products of our heredity and, especially, our environment.

> Menninger sees rehabilitation as a replacement for the concept of justice in criminal procedure: The very word *justice* irritates scientists. No surgeon expects to be asked if an operation for cancer is just or not. No doctor will be reproached on the grounds that the dose of penicillin he has prescribed is less or more than *justice* would stipulate. . . . It does not advance a solution to use the word *justice*. It is a subjective emotional word. . . . The concept is so vague, so distorted in its application, so hypocritical, and usually so irrelevant that it offers no help in the solution of the crime problem which it exists to combat but results in its exact opposite—injustice, injustice to everybody.[25]

---

25. Karl Menninger, *The Crime of Punishment* (Viking Press, 1968), 17, 10–11. The passage is remarkable for its apparent denial and assertion of the objective reality of justice.

There practical wisdom, what the Greeks called *phronesis* is needed. A uniform schedule of penalties for various crimes attempts to provide standardized punishments, removing arbitrariness from the penal system; but the weakness of this system is that it also removes discretion, *phronesis,* from the sentencing process.

Finally, we must separate retributivism from vengeance. Vengeance signifies acts that arise out of the victims' desire for revenge, for satisfying their anger at the criminal for what he or she has done. The nineteenth-century British philosopher James Fitzjames Stephen thought this was a justification for punishment, arguing that punishment should be inflicted "for the sake of gratifying the feeling of hatred—call it revenge, resentment, or what you will—which the contemplation of such [offensive] conduct excites in healthily constituted minds."[21] But retributivism is not based on hatred for the criminal (though a feeling of vengeance may accompany the punishment). Retributivism is the theory that the criminal *deserves* to be punished and deserves to be punished in proportion to the gravity of his or her crime—whether or not the victim or anyone else desires it. We may all deeply regret having to carry out the punishment.

On the other hand, people do have a sense of outrage and passion for revenge at criminals for their crimes. Stephen was correct in asserting that "[t]he criminal law stands to the passion for revenge in much the same relation as marriage to the sexual appetite."[22] Failure to punish would no more lessen our sense of vengeance than the elimination of marriage would lessen our sexual appetite. When a society fails to punish criminals in a way thought to be proportionate to the gravity of the crime, the public is likely to take the law into its own hands, resulting in vigilante justice, lynch mobs, and private acts of retribution. The outcome is likely to be an anarchistic, insecure state of injustice.

Although the retributivist theory has broad intuitive appeal, it is not without problems. One problem is to make sense out of the notion of balancing the scales of justice. The metaphor suggests a cosmic scale which is put out of balance by a crime, but such a scale might not exist, or if one does, it may not be our duty to maintain it through punishment. That may

---

21. Sir James Fitzjames Stephen, *Liberty, Equality, Fraternity* (Cambridge University Press, 1867), 152.

22. Sir James Fitzjames Stephen, *A History of Criminal Law in England* (Macmillan, 1863), 80.

be God's role. Furthermore, retributivism seems unduly retrospective. If we can restore the repentant criminal to moral integrity through rehabilitative processes, then to insist on a pound of flesh seems barbaric. Nevertheless, although retributivism needs to be supplemented by other considerations, it still provides the core idea of justice as distribution on the basis of desert. It will be the basis of my defense of capital punishment in the next part of this work.

Utilitarian Theories

Utilitarian theories are theories of deterrence, reform, and prevention. The emphasis is not on the gravity of the evil done, but on deterring and preventing future evil. Their motto might be, "Don't cry over spilt milk!" Unlike retributive theories which are backward-looking and based on *desert*, Utilitarian theories are *forward*-looking, based on social improvement. Jeremy Bentham (1748–1832) and John Stuart Mill (1806–1873) are classic Utilitarians. Their position can be analyzed into three theses:

1. Social utility (including reform, prevention, and deterrence) is a necessary condition for judicial punishment.
2. Social utility is a sufficient condition for judicial punishment.
3. The proper amount of punishment to be imposed upon the offender is that amount which will do the most good (or least harm) to all those who will be affected by it.

Stanley Benn puts it well: "The margin of increment of harm inflicted on the offender should be preferable to the harm avoided by fixing that penalty rather than one slightly lower."[23]

Punishment is a technique of social control, justified so long as it prevents more evil than it produces. If there is a system of social control that will give a greater balance (e.g., rehabilitation), then the utilitarian will opt for that. The utilitarian doesn't accept Draconian laws that would deter because the punishment would be worse than the crime, causing greater suffering than the original offense. Only three grounds are permissible for punishment: (1) to prevent a repetition; (2) to deter others—the threat of

---

23. Stanley Benn, "Punishment," in *The Encyclopedia of Philosophy,* ed. Paul Edwards (Macmillan, 1967), 29–35.

punishment deters potential offenders; and (3) to rehabilitate the criminal (this need not be seen as punishment, but it may involve that).

The threat of punishment is everything. Every act of punishment is to that extent an admission of the failure of the threat. If the threat were successful, no punishment would be needed, and the question of justification would not arise.

One problem with the utilitarian theory is simply that it goes against our notion of desert. It says that social utility is a necessary condition for punishment. But I would be in favor of punishing at least the most egregious offenders even if I knew they would never commit another crime. Suppose we discovered Adolf Hitler living quietly in a small Argentine town and were sure that no good (in terms of deterrence or prevention) would come of punishing him. Shouldn't we still bring him to trial and punish him appropriately?

A further problem is that utilitarianism would seem to enjoin punishment for prospective crimes. If the best evidence we have leads us to believe that some person or group of people will commit a crime, we are justified in applying punitive measures if our actions satisfy a cost-benefit analysis.

The main weakness of utilitarianism is that it seems to allow the punishment of the innocent if that will deter others from crime. We want only criminals punished, but utilitarians focus on results, not justice. If we can frame an innocent bum for a rape and murder in order to prevent a riot, the utilitarian will be tempted to do so. This violates the essence of justice.

Some philosophers, namely Anthony Quinton, Stanley Benn, and R. S. Peters, have rejected this criticism as missing the point of what punishment is. They contend that punishment is logically connected with committing a crime, so that the one punished must be presumed guilty.[24] But this "definitional stop" only moves the problem to a different dimension with-

---

24. Anthony Quinton, "Punishment," in *Philosophy, Politics and Society*, ed. P. Laslett, 1959; Stanley Benn and R. S. Peters admit that "If utilitarianism could really be shown to involve punishing the innocent, or a false parade of punishment, or punishment in anticipation of an offense, these criticisms would no doubt be conclusive. They are, however, based on a misconception of what the utilitarian theory is about. We said at the beginning of this chapter that 'punishment' implied in its primary sense, not the inflicting of *any* sort of suffering, but inflicting suffering under certain specified conditions, one of which was that it must be for a breach of a rule" ("The Utilitarian Case for Deterrence," 98).

There practical wisdom, what the Greeks called *phronesis* is needed. A uniform schedule of penalties for various crimes attempts to provide standardized punishments, removing arbitrariness from the penal system; but the weakness of this system is that it also removes discretion, *phronesis,* from the sentencing process.

Finally, we must separate retributivism from vengeance. Vengeance signifies acts that arise out of the victims' desire for revenge, for satisfying their anger at the criminal for what he or she has done. The nineteenth-century British philosopher James Fitzjames Stephen thought this was a justification for punishment, arguing that punishment should be inflicted "for the sake of gratifying the feeling of hatred—call it revenge, resentment, or what you will—which the contemplation of such [offensive] conduct excites in healthily constituted minds."[21] But retributivism is not based on hatred for the criminal (though a feeling of vengeance may accompany the punishment). Retributivism is the theory that the criminal *deserves* to be punished and deserves to be punished in proportion to the gravity of his or her crime—whether or not the victim or anyone else desires it. We may all deeply regret having to carry out the punishment.

On the other hand, people do have a sense of outrage and passion for revenge at criminals for their crimes. Stephen was correct in asserting that "[t]he criminal law stands to the passion for revenge in much the same relation as marriage to the sexual appetite."[22] Failure to punish would no more lessen our sense of vengeance than the elimination of marriage would lessen our sexual appetite. When a society fails to punish criminals in a way thought to be proportionate to the gravity of the crime, the public is likely to take the law into its own hands, resulting in vigilante justice, lynch mobs, and private acts of retribution. The outcome is likely to be an anarchistic, insecure state of injustice.

Although the retributivist theory has broad intuitive appeal, it is not without problems. One problem is to make sense out of the notion of balancing the scales of justice. The metaphor suggests a cosmic scale which is put out of balance by a crime, but such a scale might not exist, or if one does, it may not be our duty to maintain it through punishment. That may

---

21. Sir James Fitzjames Stephen, *Liberty, Equality, Fraternity* (Cambridge University Press, 1867), 152.

22. Sir James Fitzjames Stephen, *A History of Criminal Law in England* (Macmillan, 1863), 80.

be God's role. Furthermore, retributivism seems unduly retrospective. If we can restore the repentant criminal to moral integrity through rehabilitative processes, then to insist on a pound of flesh seems barbaric. Nevertheless, although retributivism needs to be supplemented by other considerations, it still provides the core idea of justice as distribution on the basis of desert. It will be the basis of my defense of capital punishment in the next part of this work.

Utilitarian Theories

Utilitarian theories are theories of deterrence, reform, and prevention. The emphasis is not on the gravity of the evil done, but on deterring and preventing future evil. Their motto might be, "Don't cry over spilt milk!" Unlike retributive theories which are backward-looking and based on *desert*, Utilitarian theories are *forward*-looking, based on social improvement. Jeremy Bentham (1748–1832) and John Stuart Mill (1806–1873) are classic Utilitarians. Their position can be analyzed into three theses:

1. Social utility (including reform, prevention, and deterrence) is a necessary condition for judicial punishment.
2. Social utility is a sufficient condition for judicial punishment.
3. The proper amount of punishment to be imposed upon the offender is that amount which will do the most good (or least harm) to all those who will be affected by it.

Stanley Benn puts it well: "The margin of increment of harm inflicted on the offender should be preferable to the harm avoided by fixing that penalty rather than one slightly lower."[23]

Punishment is a technique of social control, justified so long as it prevents more evil than it produces. If there is a system of social control that will give a greater balance (e.g., rehabilitation), then the utilitarian will opt for that. The utilitarian doesn't accept Draconian laws that would deter because the punishment would be worse than the crime, causing greater suffering than the original offense. Only three grounds are permissible for punishment: (1) to prevent a repetition; (2) to deter others—the threat of

23. Stanley Benn, "Punishment," in *The Encyclopedia of Philosophy*, ed. Paul Edwards (Macmillan, 1967), 29–35.

punishment deters potential offenders; and (3) to rehabilitate the criminal (this need not be seen as punishment, but it may involve that).

The threat of punishment is everything. Every act of punishment is to that extent an admission of the failure of the threat. If the threat were successful, no punishment would be needed, and the question of justification would not arise.

One problem with the utilitarian theory is simply that it goes against our notion of desert. It says that social utility is a necessary condition for punishment. But I would be in favor of punishing at least the most egregious offenders even if I knew they would never commit another crime. Suppose we discovered Adolf Hitler living quietly in a small Argentine town and were sure that no good (in terms of deterrence or prevention) would come of punishing him. Shouldn't we still bring him to trial and punish him appropriately?

A further problem is that utilitarianism would seem to enjoin punishment for prospective crimes. If the best evidence we have leads us to believe that some person or group of people will commit a crime, we are justified in applying punitive measures if our actions satisfy a cost-benefit analysis.

The main weakness of utilitarianism is that it seems to allow the punishment of the innocent if that will deter others from crime. We want only criminals punished, but utilitarians focus on results, not justice. If we can frame an innocent bum for a rape and murder in order to prevent a riot, the utilitarian will be tempted to do so. This violates the essence of justice.

Some philosophers, namely Anthony Quinton, Stanley Benn, and R. S. Peters, have rejected this criticism as missing the point of what punishment is. They contend that punishment is logically connected with committing a crime, so that the one punished must be presumed guilty.[24] But this "definitional stop" only moves the problem to a different dimension with-

---

24. Anthony Quinton, "Punishment," in *Philosophy, Politics and Society*, ed. P. Laslett, 1959; Stanley Benn and R. S. Peters admit that "If utilitarianism could really be shown to involve punishing the innocent, or a false parade of punishment, or punishment in anticipation of an offense, these criticisms would no doubt be conclusive. They are, however, based on a misconception of what the utilitarian theory is about. We said at the beginning of this chapter that 'punishment' implied in its primary sense, not the inflicting of *any* sort of suffering, but inflicting suffering under certain specified conditions, one of which was that it must be for a breach of a rule" ("The Utilitarian Case for Deterrence," 98).

out solving it. Suppose we call "punishment" punishing the guilty and give another name, such as "telishment" (Rawls's suggestion), to judicially harming the innocent for deterrent purposes. Now the question becomes "Should we ever telish people?" The utilitarian is committed to telishment—whenever the aggregate utility warrants it.

While these criticisms are severe, they do not overthrow utilitarianism altogether. One surely admits that penal law should have a deterrent effect. The point seems to be that utilitarian theories need a retributive base on which to build. I will comment on this point later.

Rehabilitative Theories

According to rehabilitative theories, crime is a disease, and the criminal is a sick person who needs to be cured, not punished. Such rehabilitationists as B. F. Skinner, Karl Menninger, and Benjamin Karpman point to the failure and cruelties of our penal system and advocate an alternative of therapy and reconditioning. "Therapy not torture" might be said to be their motto for criminals are not really in control of their behavior but are suffering personality disorders. Crime is, by and large, a result of an adverse early environment, so that what must be done is to recondition the criminal through positive reinforcement. Punishment is a prescientific response to antisocial behavior. At best punishment temporarily suppresses adverse behavior, but, if untreated, Skinner argues, it will resurface again as though the punishment never occurred. It is useless as a deterrent. Rehabilitationists charge that retributivists are guilty of holding an antiquated notion of human beings as possessing free wills and being responsible for their behavior. We, including all of our behavior, are all products of our heredity and, especially, our environment.

> Menninger sees rehabilitation as a replacement for the concept of justice in criminal procedure: The very word *justice* irritates scientists. No surgeon expects to be asked if an operation for cancer is just or not. No doctor will be reproached on the grounds that the dose of penicillin he has prescribed is less or more than *justice* would stipulate. . . . It does not advance a solution to use the word *justice*. It is a subjective emotional word. . . . The concept is so vague, so distorted in its application, so hypocritical, and usually so irrelevant that it offers no help in the solution of the crime problem which it exists to combat but results in its exact opposite—injustice, injustice to everybody.[25]

---

25. Karl Menninger, *The Crime of Punishment* (Viking Press, 1968), 17, 10–11. The passage is remarkable for its apparent denial and assertion of the objective reality of justice.